LINES THROUGH

LINES THROUGH

JOEL MITCHELL
ROB FONTELLA
JOHN HAWKINSON
NORA BONNER
DAN ROTH

SEETALK *CHICAGO*
2008

First Edition

Library of Congress Cataloging-in-Publication Data

Mitchell, Joel; Fontella-Zajkowski, Robert
Lines Through

ISBN: 978-0-6152-1706-2

Cover Design by Rob Fontella

Printed and bound in the United States

Seetalk 6026 N. Winthrop, Chicago 60660

Contents

Preface

We were at the Ernie Pub, a bar in Hawk's basement built by his father in the 50's. Rough hewn birch and bright mirrors. I told Hawk, "You know you're responsible for this."

"For what?" he asked.

"For this," I said, with my hand on the pages that are now in yours.

Years before I'd given him a copy of Federico Garcia Lorca's *In Search of Duende* and then in turn he gave me a copy of *The Theory and Practice of River's* by Jim Harrison. While in a performance of *Henry V* we had introduced each other to beautiful giants. That was where this book began and grew, in the midst of friendship.

Later I got my hands on *Braided Creek*, the poetic exchange between Harrison and Ted Kooser. And while Rob was in South America I sent him, All Out of Glue, a poem. He sent another one right back. And I asked if he wanted to start a braided conversation. His answer: we'd already begun. Our exchange continued for two years and is nestled in the middle of this book.

The *ghazals* were all written in one month, the month of March last year, a month in the northern United States given to climactic leaps and reversals and so appropriate to the form. There can be snow on the ground, rain sheeting on windows, and at the same time sun. One wins and then they're all gone. Our interpretation of the *ghazal* also comes from Jim Harrison. Thank you.

And this collection concludes with spontaneous braids, as if somewhere in their center there was a magnet and then the words came, expressions stuck together, poem built on poem, voice upon voice.

At the center of these exchanges was an open in-between that inspired discovery and risk. Come in. Then start your own and raise a glass with friends. Cheers.

2008

Ghazals

I.

drifts of ice chunks float like dead skin on the river as
the cool concrete burns right through my shoes.

i only know the alphabet if i sing it all the way through
aside from that i might as well be thinking greek.

we rolled together in a field of dandelions: white and yellow
as her skirt lifted slightly i began to dream of weeds.

pain is always on the inside whether physical or not
once it reaches the outside it becomes joy.

grace. grace was fed to me tremendously in the seventies
unfortunately i hid it under the table never to be regained.

i overheard a sick bird complaining to a friend about the end
and how even in the next life he'll have to have wings.

M.

II.

i've walked on these boards before, laughing, crying, singing
in the skin of beggars, liars, thieves, and priests.

the cap twisted off, that should have been enough of a clue
as all the wine spilled out like the blood of Christ on sinners.

"hurry up and cook the eggs!" exclaimed a red faced Maria
"i can't bear the thought of them turning into chickens."

i found a stain on an old shirt of mine (placed right over the heart)
i got that stain while riding with you... it won't, it won't wash out.

the pier was in a permanent state of drench, all the world crashed
into the wall and separated into the mist hitting my cheeks.

III.

big fat drops of rain, thick snow sinking into the grass, lashing wind
the sun erupts and then is smothered gray

take the elevator down, walk across the parking lot, look through the fence
and still not see the names on the stones, that much i can do from here

trees look like black coral, the planes: fish, the sea: gray
i can breathe everywhere except in mirrors

we should float our pink lawn flamingos to Cuba as a gesture of turning over
our secrets. release them here and see if they'll go on their own

she had a black umbrella, told me she found it on the el. told her about mine
from my father. and she said it sounded like a woman's cuz' a the colors

IV.

she looked like someone else from behind, wouldn't of understood
my question about getting bit by a german shepherd

i'm going to invent a medical condition, something Minoan
that will fit on a vase and be broken by a cure

when we were on the submarine everything was fine
it's on the surface that the rain mattered

one plus one, again, equals infinity, it's just
there's nowhere to spend it

another miracle? hold my eyes open so i can dream while awake
a ham sandwich has made me as sleepy as a can of tomatoes

V.

the lake and the sky are in love

they share each other's thoughts

Gavrilo, if my President drove through Sarajevo

a turning circle would be enough

their voices were like water, “buiwp, buiwp,” into a copper well

which left the tent before i could drown

he’s a mouse named Herbert. she’s a goldfish named Claudia

they lived in my imagination, and woulda met but for the cat

i always thought there was someplace better

until i got here. but then you left

F.

VI.

riding on the elevated train, it's circular here

you can never get to where you weren't.

hair clings to my neck, temples, & cheeks

i swear it wasn't going to rain today.

gone fishin! don't really know my pocket

i can't believe that's what i did last night.

a red headed child gave me her last candy

make me to know what it is to serve others.

i had a black cat who died from the cancer

nobody cried but i heard Bob Dylan moan.

VII.

the wind is saying something, always with an h. could be
“who,” how,” or “why.” until it’s done we can’t be sure

he moves as if to show her he’s become a man: a son
with his mother. stamp from the roll, thumb on envelope

in a dream the Mariner weaves
a tale of looking without love

“ice cream is like truth,” the fork said to the spoon
while the bent knife looked on

NAPLES: hand grenade in the potatoes, where am i from?
they think France, blown-up in a park all gone

F.

VIII.

The *salaa* outside is under repair

I hope to perfect rest before he comes.

Kreuntep a'ha nakorn means "pure city."

We watch the air and wonder who to blame.

"Keep watch, don't sleep tonight," he cries to me.

I just want to fall asleep in your lap.

I shook hands with *Muang Thai* in August.

It's been August for over seven months.

Be on your guard; to doze off is to die.

Boredom's reserved for him who won't notice.

IX.

the roofs shone silver and the tops of wings flashed white

outside came in today and then shied away

i know that trees warm each other even under

the snow. that's how i want to be with you

sunlight eased up the windows in one long exhalation

copper in golden blossom, then flames drained amber away

we'd married, divorced, mended, had children; sighs, tears,

smiles, disputes—then none! all before she even wrote back

moon

are you my friend?

F.

X.

he thought of stories and poems as people with personalities

and it was his father who started filling his room with friends

the bear scat was fresh. they only had a few apples

they portaged over the sand bar when the moon rose

the Mandans would cut off finger tips

as a display of grief. i was born a crab

the words that fall into place are not to hold

back water, but swim in a common sea

my street could play the game of license plates

so many other states. are they still made by inmates?

XI.

Six A.M. brown and white Mini in Viking Purple as the Sun shrugs off its moon. Six P.M. baby in my arms, pink and peach, laughing 'til I can't breathe

He went back to Texas a little less cowboy, a little more woman. She went to Oregon in a ten gallon hat with a pint of beer and her back teeth floating

Human nature is an invention of mankind, ever expansive

Ever notice how nature doesn't need excuses for murder

I lull myself into a concentrated mind of disillusionment

Excited to sleep

Dear hope, do you mention me in your future plans?

I sometimes depend on you for a smile

R.

XII.

the bridge buckled and splintered covered with
band-aids, a soul is not required to feel pain.

the only thing we really caught was a hangover
but that one little fish just flipped and flopped.

i was so caught up in my own cleverness that
all the bills were late. extra fees ain't clever.

the sun and the moon really had a tussle this
morning, i just hid under the covers till it passed.

i wrote and wrote... really taking a shit for the soul,
i hope i don't start commenting on myself.

XIII.

the wind pushes away the sun and the waves break

through the building's lengthening blue shadow

"without light," he wrote, "the world would be flat"

that's not right. he wrote, "shadows"

an epic seen all at once

would be but a single point

mirrors have no memory

until they're broken

my heart is useless

unless it's making love

XIV.

The world clicks around the side streets in new heels.

She shakes her way into another week.

The sky blurs into the concrete forest.

I want and need and need and want. and Want. and Need.

Another mystery sprawls out on the lazy boy.

She flips the channels and ignores our questions.

A fish, a cat, a duck, and a guitar: *farang* curiosity .

Where does Mexico find the time to dance?

There are gym shoes, taxis, and staplers in every color.

The rainbow left its lover in the bathtub smoking cloves.

XV.

sir! yes sir! i've checked my gun and my pack
now you can't make me murder.

butter, garlic, onions, peppers, pork, & cumin
stir over fire and serve to the righteous.

i walked on the water till it turned to wine
now i'm buried next to fishes.

her eyes weren't as blue as the sky but
surely they were much wider.

i bit and scratched my way to the bottom of
the glass, better send for reinforcements.

M.

XVI.

sega krad wen a fo nwad eht no

stnemidnoc ylno dna .yrgnuh .m.a eerht

we will overcome!

look at navel oranges

wicker basket smelling of rain water

no handles, full of bricks

i have a limousine so big that to turn the key

would drain the world of its gasoline

the radiator sounds like a wounded raft. to beat

the sea at its own game i open the window

worms sleeping in the garden

angels float on Chicago's appetite

XVII.

Okay so this guy

He gets stranded in this nowheres town

The families all go on like nothing's changed, nothing's happened

But each ones got like a secret hatred of one another

They kiss and the husband comes in

Four years later they'll both be divorced, he's tryin to find her

It's an all out chase scene

Helicopter, trucks, high speed, all that shit

Turns out she was the one who was hiding it

Three years later they're in the tropics

XVIII.

in a fever i saw the Father, Son, and the Holy Ghost

i wish i had prepared a cake a pie or something.

a wise afghani told me to melt myself like snow

where did all this dirt come from?

i never really had a truly spectacular peach

this whole fruit business is a pack of lies.

a wise jew told me to love all the world

where did all this trouble come from?

i never climbed a mountain because it was there

my head is rarely in the clouds.

XIX.

recycling great. but watch the salesmen

yesterday will be at tomorrow's prices

i boasted they teach trapeze over there. "i'd love to learn trapeze,"

she sighed. but to me it's just what *plugra* tells you about a grocery store

Plato is jealous that truth is not persuasive by itself

long time jealous now. woof, woof. apple falls on head

they still ate horse meat at Harvard in the 70's

the glue factory. money stuck to ideas

let's make a board game called *Casa Real*, meaning: royal

in Spanish, real in English. it would be like strip poker

F.

XX.

all the excuses have been used up

i love you all the same.

love is a hammer i never used to swing

nails have always wondered why.

bring another gin to the table

Bond thought vodka made martinis.

when her skirt hid her thighs from light

shame was something taught not found.

the captain had a Gulliver-sized head

my brain never questioned God.

XXI.

i hope to be healthy, wealthy and wise

and gentle… somehow gentle too

O my America, 1000 new perfumes

same stench. vomit in your shoes

yesterday—warm. last night—blank. today—waiting

the sky wrapped as a pharaoh of plundered grave

clocks keep their faces and hands behind glass

before that there had been too many robberies

she said, "they made fun of me"

"death," he said, "does make us feel stupid"

the moon is too primitive a paradise for wind

Baudrillard will never always have died

F.

XXII.

mirror shard mosaics wink from temples

lots of something for the man who worshipped nothing

minimal centimeters measure her cherry tree lips and ivory arms

please consider these girls' bones when making love to them

mischief sleeps without underwear beneath a black comforter

another hometown rejects its prophet

mutt bitches fight over mango peels

lungs adapt to mountain air

mirrors sway in white-sand hammocks sipping rum

narcissus learns to meditate

XXIII.

she had sand... character... beauty... grace...

but she only ever wanted to be a star.

wires were crossed under the Indian Ocean

those waves took back my soul.

holiday trappings lingering way too long

i cornered her under the Arbor Day mistletoe.

two colombian sisters, one like coffee the other

like cocaine... both keep me up at night.

i went pocket fishing again the other night

why is it so easy to steal from yourself.

XXIV.

workers, lovers, fiends, surging up the stairs. eager. competent

from the 921 at 7:34. sunlight chopping sunlight steps

a friend, yes, the kind that could show up

in a dream. but not the kind you could tell

my credit card keeps my hand warm

so red it glows

tell me the name of that building, and that one, wonderful

can we go inside, towards the echo of it being built

amore ad ovum sino quo proctor hoc

co-co-ri-co poulet documentento

XXV.

where i am from is where i am

it's a circle i never quite fit inside

i draw hope with a heart and over the i

in your name. over and over down the page

Bad Love Vol. Next: meekness, her weakness, her weapon

she bottomless hunger hangs limp from the last of his smile

we are flesh. we are builders. who

laid tracks over our temples, our toes?

Carlos has landed in Cali today and no longer needs

the worn *foto* he kept like a map to a private treasure

F.

XXVI.

From now on I will look at no advertisement, none

Food's only representation should be a fork and knife

I'm glad Bush shuts his mouth about Chavez

How can we talk, everyone breaks eggs in omelet making

There are places on this earth where thousands of square miles are covered in sea grass. This place is called Sharks Bay and it is in Australia

It has been harder and harder to leave my bed in the mornings

Maybe I suffer from some kind of disease

If you never spoke out of turn or unpreparedly

How could you be ready when the proper time comes?

R.

XXVII.

my heart is an enormous field of cactuses

for moisture i tapped one of the many cacti.

kisses, waves, & tears on the JC Lodge

she floated away today.

he shifted his thin ass on the sleek divan

this store oughta be called the dumpster.

eyes heavy from all the manufactured

energy, i rest my head at *casa de petra.*

i used to be described by adults as ornery

these days, i'm not bothered by much.

+

sweat halos my head

as neruda weeps saintly

all the leaves have thawed

M.

XXIII.

the bark of the date palm is a crusty shield which
shelters a broken city drowning in baby's tears.

the sun was a shy mermaid peering through
the icy surface of clouds... unrequited.

he squeezed so much out of that damn bean
that eventually the brown water never worked.

spent all night with gauges measuring love and hate
i should know (i am an expert) how to treat people.

such a wondrous landscape around every turn with
my eyes kissing the sensual lips of flowers.

XXIX.

red wine pouring out the first sky

sitting backwards on the train

i learned how to read the gauges

properly, expertly, three quarters empty

a rock floated by the grieving side

of the island on a slab of ice

there are cries of intolerance!

when foreigners no speaka da guiltish

the blind man came to watch thoughts grow into wishes

and now memory is tended by volunteer in a glass house

F.

XXX.

i see the dirt on the top of my shoes

when my posture is bent under heavy thoughts

now, there's no death penalty in *Sepharad*

except for bulls. my family ran with their name

Leonardo's thoughts were written upstream:

"evom ton seod ti ,nus eht"

Lindbergh/America: great courage, ransom for a dead baby

photo-op with murderers, machine hung from the ceiling

on the grass, on the debris from the great fire

the sympathy plays in Frank Gehry's pavilion

XXXI.

all the air is clogged by sunshine and smiles

i overheard two birds plotting my destruction.

i longed for her hips and that small stretch of

fabric, i couldn't concentrate on moving pawns

the flowers were streaked with rain and dirt

they didn't realize that they were born in Toledo.

sthkt, sthkt, sthkt… no more scratchy blues

someone turn the album over please.

the fish soup was quickly dispatched

some escaped onto a corner of my shirt.

M.

XXXII.

i'd held my anger under so it couldn't breathe, water went cloudy, bottom

choked without complaint and the surface reflected strangers before me

everyone is not everyone anymore, but byronic flesh lashed to

byronic bones. animated torches. flames of green leaves.

she said she should be doing work but was reading

"this instead." poetry

blue water, blue sky, blue eyes. then clouds, ice, and blinking

blinking buoyant days. flash bulbs creasing shadows

in a dream, so much volume came out of my throat

that a motorcycle's get away went unheard

XXXIII.

carried away from a small patch of earth

we learn to hate... we learn to be violent...

let the rain collect for a while on my head

it's unusually warm for this time of year.

i caught a moth in the palm of my hand

does that mean that i possess light?

shoulder low, i burst through the wall!

did someone call for kool-aid?

i found her in each tap of the keyboard

always finding a new rhythm.

XXXIV.

Clever titles sometimes drop me at such a place that progress cannot be made

I stand at the foot of the Yellow Brick and cannot hop the fist skip

As the day moped on we mingled body parts under slick sheets

We couldn't hear the rain but could feel it was there

Guilt eats at my stomach like nervousness's little brother

My sticky hand covered in bark and dirt after leaving the honeycomb empty

Telling someone they are not smart and need to be smarter

doesn't have any positive effect. Come on, you're smarter than that

You shouldn't take pride in finishing something

That you took no pride in doing

XXXV.

i remember eating dinner with the family, 6 sharp

the phone would ring and dad would bellow: "buzz off!"

perspective can really shift and shuffle like waves

i stepped out of my skull and found a new way to love.

bright outside... i can tell by looking at this screen

reflected from a sign: "we buy ugly houses."

shift to the right, shift to the left, up down spin

can't hear the awful lyrics when i'm just shakin it.

a mexican just fixed our water purifier machine thing

oh how the tables have turned!

M.

XXXVI.

i am here, my idol the sun

is eight and a half minutes behind

she blew the bridge, he drained the water

over the earth and pillows they reigned

it's all about the tortoise and the hare

if races can be won

he wants to ask one hundred and fifty women what is love

while he runs away from one, a Greek named Olga

i sighed to imagine their paired love

masturbating each other from their wheelchairs

XXXVII.

"The Irish saved civilization"

"Aye, so they are blaming us for that too, are they?"

if the sea were the heart, and tides its pulse, and if the mind

were the wind and gusts its thoughts, my navel is the bath tub

the river changes directions between day and night between dark

and light, and in a few hours we'll have drown dizzy overwhelmed

for luck, throw women over one shoulder

and men over the other, salt accordingly

these are some of the hottest days of the year i swear

outside can't keep up with the alligators

F.

XXXVIII.

"well jimmy played harmonica in the pub where
i was born," everyone is irish tomorrow.

visited a tea house where people read on stage
while playing music… Curly's wife had red hair.

i've learned a good many things over the years
firstly, don't throw-up on your friends.

saw a rainbow while riding shotgun in a car
the pot of gold sat squarely in my lap.

told my girl that i loved her and someone
overheard… embarrassment is just silly.

XXXIX.

it used to be if i sat very still, time would not move
then the notices for jury duty stopped coming too

the phone cord got tangled all around. no one
to hit or throw things at, or even pry for a kiss

the freighters have started moving again
yesterday made one, today makes two

he could get 75 years for disrespecting a Thai photo
grapher. Bhumibol, may dead fish rain upon you!

Richard they are talking about Chicago now. how
important it was before you left and wrote haikus

F.

XL.

watching a green fern grow and thrive

roots all tangled in a jar for kosher pickles.

thought about the feel of skin under fingertips

it's almost light now and the cars are heading home.

truth wore a mask & held a red, white & blue cross

i decided honesty was better but cost more $$$$$

eyes closed and stretched flat in the middle of a

lake, don't know how but i've learned to float.

arms wrists & ankles twisted all together in love

the sirens and alarms sound like music.

XLI.

Someone said 'If you accomplish your goals, they weren't big enough'

Hey, buddy, you ever hear of early retirement?

The office pleads with me, begging me

Okay fine, I'll push your plastic buttons

I try to keep things civil, professional even

But as I sit here there is animal thirsting inside of me

What if the trees decided not to grow leafs this year?

Who would be the first to notice?

In the wee hours, when I whispered of my lazy secret

You laid there, stroking my arm, and admitted you too loved the snooze button

XLII.

bright dirty sun

bright dirty

where people are

most

the vodka pint

passed till M-T

matter

matters

sleeping backwards

awake forgetting

F.

XLIII.

i live in a puzzle and God

dropped some of the pieces on his oriental carpet

months are long days and years are summer minutes

in Michigan. just one goddamn cigarette, please

i gotta find that button that changes my laptop to thainglish

i gotta find that button in my own brain

all lotion is whitening lotion. all models are white

drink milk while you're pregnant and you will get white babies

terror. terrific. terrible. territory.

your ancestors is complicate!

B.

XLIV.

pull the collar close and breath through
cold teeth, the sun is a liar.

i can't keep all this information straight
there's a disc in my drive and my back.

she unleashed the fury of her colors
and i wished hard that i was crayola.

i dreamed i was on an island with palms
now all i want is coconut cream pies.

ants crawl all over a green leaf in spring
god made tools for monkeys & water on mars.

XLV.

i can't rewind the news. did they say

they found a way to get the blood out?

this is baseball weather, out of the park

but i'm thankless. it's how it should always be

indolent suggests work is close to pain

go ahead, wear yourself out, name calling

there is nothing to nothing about. coupons

road construction, carnations, water on fire

i agree with you. the politic-y talk sounds like a…ah…a

commercial break, back to the ah… after a… stick around

nice to meet you too, let's keep busy

until it gets dark then screw

XLVI.

life, liberty and moving boxes. that came to me in a dream

over and over until i woke up repeating it

my open heartache satellite has got a chameleon crew

and dresses up for its own holidays

who's really in there i want to ask my low calorie diet plan

wherever it went, with the money and the french fries

not walking in snow people, Albuquerque address

to whom I am "resident" your paper is no good for airplanes

i am a man without a season. it's wet, heavy, and dark

like in a vacuum cleaner in the boiler room of a steamer tug

XLVII.

i'm in a foreign land with Cash flipping me

the bird, i am my brother's keeper.

yesterday i bent two rail ties into a bow

now he's really gonna have to wait.

last night the clouds pissed on the parade

now all the lil' indians are changing clothes.

dr. Ice was blacklisted back when they did

that, he listened to his heart and brain.

napoleon just looks at me with loving eyes

we'll all have our day at Waterloo.

XLVIII.

the bus driver acts like he can't fit. but he, inching forward
does. the Straits of Gibraltar. give me a cigarette already

in the dim where candles tickle, reflexes run turnstiles over agility
and finger prints on the glass were meant to bruise the flowers

he was trying to cut finely grab-it-all on the lane
dancin' over seams, bright glare, and buzz rattle

i'd like to be more like you, Woody, your health
without skill at apology, women changing into flats

o devil dervish you're obliterated. i hit the smart bomb
one life to live. can't we negotiate

i got a letter from a pen-pal in Spain who lives in the mountains
as a child she played in Lorca's garden before it was a museum

i saw a dumpster filled with Waterloo
one's trash is another's merchandise

XLIX.

(distant) sinking all around her mind and body

with the touch of my hands to keyboard.

i knew a kid who got trapped in books

last i heard he was due for parole in 2012.

roger Hayes blows fire from his fingertips

1000 screams trapped in his paintings.

bright lights, clean stores, unbearable traffic…

what are all these dropped ceilings hiding?

people walked by dogs and governed by babies

why aren't all our flags upside down.

M.

L.

because distraction's been forced upon me

(by movies made for the a.d.d.)

because someone has the audacity to call this mess tri-seasonal

hot, hotter, and (hottest)

because all the way out here

i've got the american and they've got the dream (still)

because i'm halfway across the world for a sleepless night

thinking about my tax money (going towards that)

because because because, said Woody

(good bye good bye good bye)

B.

LI.

2008, out of Iraq… some dreams aren't worth hitting the snooze 4

more years... i can see it now: Ira8. But wait...

today's like a dog's nose. fetch!

follow the turquoise bicycle into the basement

i am reading Bovary, and that is to be said

without sneezing. the world is hollow

don't call me at this number. tell them at the switchboard you want to talk

to the locksmith and they will put you through to my house in the Keys

when i think about her

that's another lost bookmark

F.

LII.

The voice cries soulfully over the radio

I love, I love, I love

I want to move to another continent

Where everyone I meet will know something I don't

How much do you really care?

Can you care more than that?

I said what I needed to say

It was not what I wanted to hear myself say

Every day is leaf grown on the tree of life

Fall turns to winter at sometime too

LIII.

seen a red bird in a tree, song of two longs and seven shorts, morse code
for cardinal, which is code for spring, which is code for i'm a bird

i go to the doctor for pills as getting insurance
just long enough for the plates

Jesus is rising with the gas prices
the syntax is being debated

the weather is tugging on my zipper to remove my skin and blow
across the coals. and it doesn't care if i've been faithful

cutting a tree and counting the rings is proof
my heart began with a cannonball

the pen i found with you after the thaw
ran out of ink today on the word 'how'

LIV.

Love and Death hasn't come in yet. in the mean time, i can't find

a good Godot. last night watched Sleeper before bed

i cooked with a pepper saved in the freezer

since november. i don't know how i had ice

to be the last of the great sailing ships

is never as exciting as to be the first

she had heard it was nice earlier. i lied and said yes. then she ahh-d

when i described how the fog came in and swallowed the buildings

millions can stare at wood paneling and see the shape of post

industrial conspiracies. how nice. so many finished basements

LV

Fireworks explode in the sky next to my head, off the bluff

She led him to a comfortable couch, past the trees, past the farm

The life of a blue whale is at least 80 years

Until the 35 Remington is brought out from behind the bar

He went to the shore on the eve of his death

The night yields angels that will make you sad

A place to lay his head, and drift off, into his eternal sleep

Like our brother the bear, going off away, deep into the woods

I pulled him from the daffodils, that Sunday morning, to find his peace

More than a nephew, a brother to share, your blood and sorrow

The 4th day in July found me lying on my couch

Listening to the hundred highways that I would travel for the first time

With all my strength, I couldn't move my nephew while he was alive

Yet now I carry his ashes, in but one of my arms

LVI.

woke up with an apple and some yogurt

what will i do to end suffering today?

standing halfway in the calm blue river

all of nature working together for silence.

i wear my father like a mask

Gilbert & Sullivan will never know it's me!

there is a mark on my ankle from a chain

i wore on an island, i wish i was there again.

i heard her laughing today, i rushed to see her

but she was already 11 hours ahead of me.

LVII.

reading struck blow by television in cubist slow-mo replay

Oswald fires from the book depository

there were people talking about the gutter again, trying to explain laughter

gutters outnumber streets two to one, unless it floods

i chewed on window sills as a child, it was a class in school

instead of recess, where they put the true believers

ever since they came out with progress there has been someone to say

"step-right-up, step right-up, hope found in bed with vanity"

there is nowhere to go when it rains, just places to stay

i dream of bigger cities, made large before the automobile

Braid

crumbling to pieces all out of glue

open the door here comes the cold

it's nowtime in detroit
don't cut yourself on the broken hearts
stone faces are smiling
they call for repentance
but i can't afford the cover and a pabst
broke in nine spots all out of glue
what holds the world together
once the duct tape dries out
i've got trouble in my eyes
and sour on my tongue
why aren't the flags upside down
whatever happened to outrage
can't find zu zu's petals all out of glue
her toes were painted silver
when the times were good
now even her smile looks like a frown and
everything she owns fits in a crumpled brown bag
a happy fuck you christmas
water seeping through the cracks all out of glue
erosion of the soul
time bitters all things to the nub
i'm gonna drink with the devil
on the day of the dead
try to speed up the process

ripped at the seams all out of glue

fear on my skin

a loaded gun's not trouble

like one that's been emptied

the moon's a hard target to miss

and no one really notices new holes

i'm all out of glue

all out of glue

got no glue

all out of glue

it dried up

or maybe wouldn't stick

pieces were dirty

maybe it was never meant to be held together

but touch like a long kiss before breaking apart

into 61 mirrors

running down the stairs

puddleing in a footstep

snagging a gum wrapper

teach me to blow a bubble

no not like that

one that won't break

tar poured into a boat to keep the water out

it stuck

the dart

only the bull's-eye ran

sinking into the sea

from the shade mending nets

they used to use fish skins to make

all out of glue

it wasn't snakes i don't think

there goes one now

like a pillow to a bird undone

my gaze made to hold

statues of passengers on the platform

flowers falling from the last car

worse than missing

is forgetting

until sharing with all you never thought to remember

she returns

on her own

like she came

a surprise

unstuck

for which you have to wait

while feeling more alone than before

61 mirrors and i can't see myself

tried all the tricks and smoke

never at the proper angle
so i'm gonna run barefoot on this concrete
until my feet find some grass
and i'll dance at the moon
to stain my feet green
leave grassy footprints all over her rooftop
while she wonders about all that racket
i'll hitch a ride on plane smoke
and drop into the stillest blue sea
shatter all reflection
her face is blue and it's hard to tell what she's thinking
looking back at the sky
a chimney sweep pulls breadcrumbs out of a winged engine
planting a gray row
it rained one drop
the jailhouse prism who promised to come back around
mill about the yard when we talk about what brought us here
until then the nights
when left to ourselves
come and go
holding back anxious horses at the gate
the fix waiting on the odds to limbo knee high to the fourth of july
up to the harvest moon and through divine almanacs
her only record played again

the ballerina cloaked in sparks
the most proximate edge of infinity tenderly plays
chicken with a slide trombone
the ventriloquist's stand-in who's rehearsing the hollow cry
falling into a more innocent revolution
and then there is that picture
the one drawn of the moon before the one of the catapult
the last one before the shadow started dancing in the trees
saying everything
spilling its own color bleeding its own perfume
and we got a box full of spares for when the sun gives out
again
and i have been called to testify
that mirrors don't lie only multiply
even when they are but seeds reaching
looking at each other
they must be the same
only one in disguise
river wearing at the rock
sea casting up the beach
butterflies and snowflakes in orbit as we come up for air
baptized in calamity the ever present new
today's voodoo 61x12
the moon is hiding

but i know all her favorite spots

she's holding back her fears

but if you whisper loud enough it becomes a scream

crows on a wire outside my window

they bicker back and forth

i know where the moon is

shouts the littlest black bird

she found a better earth to smile on

don't be ridiculous

croaks the lion crow

she's up on trial for murder

they found her with a gun

the little girl in 32b is crying for her mother

she knows how to find the moon

but can she keep her secrets safe

the crows crept in my kitchen

exhausted all my bourbon

the lion crow has got a gleam

take us to that little girl moon

we hear her cry calamity

alone again

the crows tip-toed into the hallway

that little girl never heard them coming

in my kitchen at the window

the moon is back

she's been acquitted

there's no more man in her

just a little girl who never cries

just calling over carrion

dancing dark wells

ponds without fortune

luckless reflections starving for a drop of milk

stranded cobwebs fumbling for keys to unlock the tethers

its wheels skirting red light sirens with their own rhythm sincerely intermittent

perches full of sleeping doves in full fabulous glow

behind a cloud

a steady knife

bleeding the night of its wolves

hunting from hallway corners

an empty glass that could drown a feather

the moon if you must know is the hungry eye of a giant

staring up from a frozen lake

looking for the hole into which it fell

calling out marco to the crow's polo

ghosts line the bridge with flickering prayers to icarus

while gravity gnaws below and the breeze brings a chill

the floor creaks lost pennies between the boards

the hurting makes doors open and close

people hang-up hats and put them on again

the crib becomes a toy

becomes the heart

an invisible shield battered

a ball leaking its air

a timid river under the night

but tomorrow with more heat the last drop'll go

the rocks will crack opening a new treasure

the memory of a dinosaur

once so grand it knew not fear

all other creatures cowered in its shadow of unhealed wounds

until it went to sleep weeping

so alone its jaws relaxed and dark feathers became its blanket

lips moving

the bank of my skull

is filled with elevator small talk

i don't remember how to ask for anything

i put all my prayers in a dumbwaiter

sent them up to god

they should reach him by the next century

if the lines don't give out

i lost a bet with a horse

he said the reason i work long hours is

expensive shampoo and detergent that really gets the filth out looks like i'll have to eat some crow

what do sheep count to make them sleep so innocent

doves circling overhead with a pearly gleam

they're sick and tired of stumping for peace

oily feathers stick together

hurt makes me want to go and hurt

and i have a mandate of hate from the masses

i have chipped talons and a bloody beak

the peace blue brook turning to red rapids

the thing is i don't know who to hate

man woman whoever started this

so i wait

i've set an ambush

and i wait

at night i don't light a fire

in the day i don't move

my face is painted into the background

i listen for the lies

watch for gestures

ready my rifle

looking through the sites

but i've seen too much

i don't know if i can tell anymore

so i ask

even if it's just one of you

warn me

when you are about to be cruel

i am here to help

the clouds roll in

the rains will pass

i see a flower blooming

in the eye of the butterfly

check out the resolve

as it flutters amidst the ruin

calamity does not slow the wing

fear does not dampen the color

death does not stop the soul

beauty will shine

love will roar

and i will laugh again

over november

sliding off garage tops

i remember a sinking duck

while the sea waited

fingertips resist in fists

scissors glint near shadow puppets

i remember the question well

what do you mean by better

while we talked of bullets

they gave me only one to chamber

teaching me not to be careless

i trembled in bed thinking the war had started

and death would not discriminate

i awoke in a world still breathing

and got lost

the knife

pulled the needle

of the compass

where it wanted

quiet through the snow

along a diminishing stream

toes wiggle in grass

ever sure of their footing

what do we learn from the gone

tie a shoe

skip a stone

catch a fish

all things turning color

never straining the eye

where do we go from here

take a job

find a love

bring a child

sun heat on the skin

chasing the pale away

how did we get this far

stole a dream

rode a star

broke a promise

feet now in the water

no turning back

why do birds sing

stole a fish

caught a dream

broke a love

this can't be november

the last night alone

i hold it in my hand

dreams disappear with the light

and the past could belong to anyone

maybe will get picked up

by a big jacket carrying a new shiv

the river flows to the sea

dreams disappear with the light

and the past could belong to anyone

or just lay there

a night alone

what's the future but now forgotten

dreams disappear with the light

and the past could belong to anyone

a stunned fish

a mute star

a deep dream

before she comes to my hand

and i'll take her to see

the joy factories

love to be joined

cancel the black

inspiration in the fingers

hurting the nails

heart-pain transformed

a flower drinking rain

beauty not to be seen

but felt

joy held in the hand

cancel the cold

glory in this skin

thrilling the soul

all lack erased

a new sprout finding light

beauty not to be spoken

but tasted joy

no more to be alone

wondrous rush of wind through cattails

show the hill beyond

that's sun in your hair

that raindrop the one i told you about

it hit the tree here then slid down

to this spot on the ground

it's wounded

warm breathing from just the other side of the tall grass

who moves

i cannot escape beauty

on my shoulder

though i'm in the ditch

on my hands

through useless toil

at my skull

when evil lurks within

at my heels

even when i flee

tiny reduced tiny

walking the hills

and valleys of a

single yellow rose
feet never tire on
petals
heart and mind flow
out of the blood
out of my mouth
drenching my path
letting me slide
i want to ask my father
how he came to marry
science to god
heart of gold
and mind of steel
ah the splendid glory
in all my numbered hairs
they never question why
they never ask for more
they only seek to leave me
crossing glades and rivers
walking to the sun
dropping from this golden bulb
floating back to earth
i break my harsh fall
on a single yellow rose

a footpath

a window filled with flames

opens

accepts

blood

gold

and

hair

feet fixed on tremendous rock

not on porous hope

a flame with scores of tiny windows

each opening to

truth

love

possibility

and failure

the flames jump out

licking the face

looking inside

saints shovel coal through the eyes

keeping it burning

the heart

and so i burned

harder and faster everyday

embracing my folly

drinking it down quickly

by the time i reached thirty

the needle hit e

i had no more left to give

i stayed that way for a season

now i spot a filling station

up ahead on the left

just rocks in flight

dashing through turbines

tumbled into place

with wide gaps

the long line

laid without mortar

water mixing with

soil cement skin

no glue

to stick us together

skipping along

a smooth rock dancing

from one tragedy

to the next

a wry smile about my mug

they'll never really break me

i'm waterproof

i held that hand but who led

now what is in between

bewilderment

longing

my heart blinks

is that a diving board

the pieces absently left behind come back

the what i at one time thought was everything

never belonged to me

and tomorrow

what i now know

won't be mine either

the creaks the moans the blind spots

next to the crates of polite and mysterious destructions

faces and phantoms

restless and roaming

return as well

but their elevator isn't there

when the doors open

the sun is blinding off the snow

just like her memory

it is cold

i stepped through the door

and found no floor

now my feet are soaked

and my head is sweaty

january in detroit

with riding boots and a red chair

i rushed her absent face

the end is the place to begin

for what could have been

across the chimney smoke

the outline of a pigeon

been shuffling for miles and miles

faded brown boots worn clear through

the air is wet around here

when i finally reached her tower

vacancy was the only trace of her

and so i stumbled back again

to cracked pavement and black snow

there the creature lay

matted feathers gray and white

broken beak and twisted neck

melting into dark plowed snow

a man with thirty voices and two red eyes

said that pigeon's name is chester

just another song about a bird

vacancy

empty measures fleeing at the sound

a mongoose dragging a plow

slipping into the wounds that lay fresh

on the once frontier of her smile

her bare swish of sighs

peeled laughter bark of skin surges

the drifting siege approached its reward driven to the lilac sea

fingers of dry lightening

migrations through emptiness

lips a hundred times heavy with mangrove sultry hibiscus

coughed onto the still ice

head in a bag of bad air

the idle reminder

hung on the hanger of my mute furnace

i learned to breathe bad air

heavy scented with the taste of chalk

it's all about the adjustments

mix and match lungs and the geometry of skin

if i think of her as a triangle

then it doesn't matter that i'm so square

i learned to speak with a dry mouth

caught in the throat and clipped

it's all about the will

mix and match syllables and the cost of thought
if i think of her as a word
then it doesn't matter that i don't know the
language
i learned to walk on the sea
ever shifting and frothy
it's all about faith
mix and match gravity and the law of neptune
if i think of her as a fish
then it doesn't matter that i'm drowning
between darkness and tomorrow
her attitude was just
a reflection
the gray line on a tree after a flood
bark like skin clinging to bones in a bathtub
ball bouncing in an ice cube
our worlds frozen with fear in our throats
eyelashes and moustache
warm shower to cold air
scorched moonlight
that peels right off the skin
in a moment all lost
the sun is a camera flash
days our picture

time is irrelevant outside this bar

none of the keys fit

the tumbler won't turn

it's to get out not in

i knew who i was the first time you said my name

all else washed clean away in the fury of your eye

mist covers the brain heavy

you gave me back my body but the gift was meant to keep

now i'm a stranger in my own skin

looking for directions

an empty suitcase after a long flight

in the trace of your mornings

i play your part and dress

plastic over my eyes

i didn't count the cost

letting go by littles

rather than at once

hang on saint jude

all causes are not lost

sun painted sidewalks

ready to skin the arms

of careless kids on bikes

pink painted toes

and sour iced lemonade

chase the ill away

and float down spring's river

white caps have changed direction

southern wind

i'll never sleep again

too proud to have only been born

time is my country my peacock love

centuries held in my breath waiting to be told

my cloud is lion fire with ocean feathers

blue white orange and green

seen through the trees by lightening

the river's tail holding the horizon

sky and earth blur to form my path

byways marked as rising

north was somewhere i forgot and so

i'll just ride with the sun to get my orientation

centuries held in your breath waiting to unfold

hands flecked gold from handling wings

head and blood thinned from this altitude

your course in not drenched in limitation

exhale

blue days for gray rain

slipped and hit my skin

can't get out from under

all this heavy love

breathing all the better

dry lungs and clear skull

metal on metal

rock on rock

skin on skin

fear on fear

like things shouldn't collide

out on the ocean

there is a fire

burning on the surface

in the heavens

the cool emptiness of space

inside sounds one silence

in its proportion

land heaving to

adjusting its forever

i went back to the junkyard

tried to buy back yesterday

thought i had fair value

gave the man forever

all he gave me was today

heart knows it's not fair

my rotting peach

attracting bees

ants come up the table legs

to eat without delay

will the pit behind

return an orchard

traded gravity for other wings

scratched the sky with stretched fingers

a little blood crept through

and washed away my innocence

science and faith a potent cocktail

can't fit my crimson fingers in my head

can't fix my useless feet on solid rock

can't find a place for all this knowledge

so i gave my soul to a bird

when it returns

i will be rich

i will know flight

the bird sang

but was eaten

for its meat

feathers fell away

washed in the away river

what is under that surface

trying to punch free

stealing all it touches

delivering free of charge

i'm here with lucky buoyance

deconstructing the waves

just like lovers under covers

i own my right foot right

my left foot left

they walk the plank

and i dive

i dive

my hands first

my feet last

and i plunge

can't remember when

i decided to dance

all the way across the tightrope

the joy of dancing

overturns the fear of falling

i twist my heart to find

the wounds

the gaps

the skips

all the instances covered in ignore

all the glories turned to ash

never forget

all failure starts with success

and fear should never motivate

i

had a shield

a covering

una cascara

and i begged

to have the breast plate split open

so the heart was the first skin

the nose

of the comet

solid water

night sky in my veins

determination shatters

i beg for the light

here comes thunder's cousin

starholes in the umbrella

lightening leaks

radiance in puddles shining back

lovers gazing at each other

across a table

1000 kisses in your blink

shaking all the earth

splash around in love

then hang me on the line

in all your breezes

a piñata's insides

ricocheting flames

and pierced by arrows

falling to pieces

but never rubble

always filling

but never full

butcher's tides

lovers strike

hands two

heart one

the earth would be round

even if it wasn't

in such a hurry

to be all at once

slippery walls dark with sin forgiven

dark with love's tender flakes

making balloons in the shapes of animals

thunderclaps sound of song

and strangers

losing each other in the night

over the falls and under the landings

o to be fierce
hot like concrete in august
breathe underwater
and carry the world
dance like ginger
and sing like frank
pocket the sun
and glow in the dark
temper the rage of nations
and drink up all the ocean
i'll give you
all the
answers
shatter all the earth
dream
with your eyes open

i thought
and said thanks
the sun melted
the ice off my eyes
then left for me darkness
and i slipped
on the frozen puddles
into an ocean
of sharks like me
who carry and nestle
with delicate flowers
in the deep

where we swallow
the reflection of stars
and dream
forever dream
of a surface
not broken by rain

the cold sun blistered

my warm ocean and

i forgot how to fear

my inclinations gathered

i decided this

cast off what is thrust upon

dance when there

is no moon

laugh with

tears in your mouth

love against

all this world's

hatred

i decided this

yes

all there is

is yes

but then

but then

locusts

they dream

from eggs emerge

through

sodden nets

you're right

always right

there is more

to an ocean than water

floating does wonders

for the surface

and that

the bottom

the bottom

wants to rise

to reach

to clutch

to avenge its heavy curse

dancing

enters the sky

laughter

is weightless

it is love

that heals

what the world brings

it brings

begging light

forgive me

me

but i'm scared

that freedom

is a trick

with sharp bones

and

they'll know

it's been stolen

this morning
dreamt of a tartan girl
in warrior dress
who asked me to sit on her lap

and last week i dreamed

you and i were walking

along a river bank

i think the wrong way

cause all the natives

don't know where they were native to

were walking the other way

you kept diving

in the water

then i woke up because she

moved or something

but what were you doing

in the water all that time

between
the source
and the sea

the constant motion made my skull spin

1000 negativities trapped inside 1 yes

life now with water ballooning both my lungs

the earth looks just like sky from way down here

a curse on all warmongers

they never taught me how to fly just spoke again

love is for heels

love is for heels

love is for heels

my mouth expelling like a river

i'm a statue called achilles

astride a golden fountain

sunflowers in my eyes

they splash they leap they swim they slither

i've turned them all to toads

long time toads
transformed by a spell
statue of a man
once a god
decades of broken wings
blown to the ground
a thousand thieves sinking
into the night
the marks of the war
for love
kill or be killed
hold me
he tries
she tries
to say
i am my underneath
in a red puddle
between distant shores
i would have lurched forward
out of these staining waters
had i the sand
the ability to take a life by force
but the sinews are so wrapped
along my outer skin and
trickling between each rib
of my heart's cage
holding my shoulder to my arm

and my arm to my shoulder
flowing in my disrupted bloods
and dancing in my brain's television
so much so
that i can't decipher importance or grief
flowers painted gray overthrowing love
i would have soared forward
out of these freezing waters
had i the fervor
the ability to give my life by grace
but the fingers are so twisted
sidewalks can't form the chords and
skyscrapers forgot the words
of my heart's rage
blocking the sun from my eyes
and my eyes from the sun
the empty lot's a skipping record
repeating in my brain's phonograph
so much so
that i can't find the right song
to turn the roses red again
and my soul is made for combat
to swing with every breath
on a wire strung

between fire and wave
a length of heart cord
walked in wooden shoes
with coal miner eyes
and swollen tongue
eager
and happy laughing
with a shot-gunned
spagettied chest
wounded
and walking
along a wire
strung between fire and wave
bathed in the blood of the sun
buoyant in the glow of the moon

i was built in the seventies
iron
steel
and glass
from science and music
religion minnesota
and coal pennsylvania
i was built in the seventies
dropped down from the moon
landing in a field of gasoline flowers
don't remember how to break
just plug me in and juice my soul

i was built in the seventies

never obsolete

sometimes the moon gets in my skin
and i can't remember tomorrow
only what it will bring
then it all seems to shift
like plate tectonics and divine
inspiration
i gather up my pack and sing
while the road is open
and my burden unheavy
all time leads to avenues
more or less traveled and
the tips of my fingers burn
as i turn the hands counter
so as to move forward
my pockets fill with wind
my arms are set wide
and my hard drive is full
but it's my clock that runs slow
keeping random
as icicles don't melt
but perspire
where as it's the moon that keeps its cool
visits all the nicest places
while its best friend warms the avenues
and byways during the day
and in case there is night
there are lights

that warm people far away
and warm me
seated on the melting wind
there's a curve in the air
disrupting visions
i can taste the salt in the sky
and the rain on my shoes
the sun is gray and bitchy
and the soup's gone tepid
but way back in the corner
just out of view
pipe dreams turn to reality
love settles on the foreheads
and birds aren't the only ones
who can fly
the wind comes mostly from the west

fact
the water settles in the lowest of places
the sun paints the surface warm
and at night the sky escapes
yet still some birds get lost
happy in between
weighing on the wires
and i'm glad we've all emerged
from the hollow shell of winter
corners are straightened by perfume

and the eyelashes of the least bit green
wave and tangle
reaching for open windows
and those stale framed scenes from offices
are pitched on the fire
dinosaur's footprints
laugh forgotten flags
even the concrete dances
buckles to display its stains
every bit a broken shell

i am quitting breakfast

smooth rain running

over rough glass

rough thoughts searching

over smooth legs

i am quitting breakfast

say hello to the day for me

rough telegraph
peppermill balloons
belching under
clouds on the run
soft expiration
wet newspaper
stuffed in the mouths
of bulls
sea foam blood
gasping collapse
a frayed extension cord

dangled
down a drain
arm wrestling a fuse
my money
a rubber hammer
an ironing board
used to surf

i quit breakfast
and the no use mutilation
of roosters

flash frozen
a day
fairly named piñata
needing
a clear the bleachers
hello

i never got the message

lines gave way

to shifts and cracks along

surfaces used for standing

with all the lights of treason

championing my imperfection

i had to guess

what it was you wanted

what it was you needed

what it was you gave away

a whispered word and

touch along the shoulder

an apology from deep

inside my guts

a length of rope long enough

to tie our hearts apart

i read it in the news today

you skipped for the other coast

and there is a chill that blows through space

between the electric and tele-lines

stretched over the marianas trench

where dough-boys hold for the whistle

calling them into no-man's land

sorry comes in a deck

it's never enough

of cards with girlies

to be a turtle

on the back

stepping slow

look out

there are cities

civilizations

rules of proper distance

bees playing at it with the flowers

stars in nights of pain and broken light

cold as tombs

hoot owls sharing a pint

between trains

inside out and

born to an end

the morning

spewed me out

of her hot mouth

just like the good

lord

and faith luke-warm

now i have sulfur

on my tongue

and it's hard to talk

about this and about

that

when all the world hurts

this afternoon

laughter

laughter

laughter

genuine

dizzy genuine

i am going to die

in the morning's beak

it will spit me out severed

or swallow me whole

to sing some dark

grumble quake

my guts overloaded

magpies within and magpies without

flying into the face of the sun

like matches

whispering in petrol's bloom

i'm inside out

dizzy genuine

being born

i wanted to live free of this

trade technology for dirt

and never be clean

i've pasted laughter all over my skull

and i can't find that genuine smile

at the bottom of a pint

or a turn of lorca's verse

i've sent out letters and mumbled prayers

trying to slip between

the darkness and the light

i can feel the end in every nerve

but tomorrow is all beginning

and belief is always tardy

don't know when i hopped this train

but my brain now starts to dizzy

every stop a bigger gamble

i'm afraid to jump off

crickets swallow razor blades
while their milk spreads over the moon
and cobwebs creep up a blanched egret
that peers down through the surface skim of algae
waiting for the fish to blink
and give away the vault
i drop between
and start to dig
with a pick i break through my teeth
and wearing a carbide lamp i drop down my throat
i hide behind my heart when sparking the charge

that blows apart my guts
i climb down through the bits and spread my map

out over the twitching pulp
i know it should be just ahead
but in the way that you know things that happen only once

come too far was too close

gravity help me

i leapt into the echo
the wind whistled over my ears

i'd always been mute before beauty
suddenly the cold crept up my limbs
and i was done before the bottom

that cricket lives near

the outer edge of my left ear

after a while

you don't even notice the chirp

my heart forgot the patterns

to decipher the difference

between gravity and beauty

both cause a falling

with no never mind of a landing

i looked at the map

but felt a bit dumb

i stopped having faith in cartographers

the day i got lost in my skull

chirp

i was hoping to start the journey

but i can't find my shoes

i think i left them far chirp behind

stuck in chirp the mud at the age of 7

chirp but chirp to take a step chirp

now is chirp all chirp chirp chirp

chirp chirp chirp chirp chirp chirp

chirp

an inkjet picture of a parrot

scotch taped to the electric meter

between deep shelves stocked with paprikas

chirp

spinning thirty three about and a third

the dial

chirp and chirp and chirp

while two men

talk from their registers

about how cars today get the same keys

and his was driven away

by mistake last night

chirp and chirp

a face on an appetite

the bird away in the dark

leaves fluttering down a stream

and strangers fondling

stranger's keys

the earth squeaking round

smeared over with halogen

and sobbing shadows

stones

who feel as much as we

these footprints

can only be followed

back from where they came

dwindling free

the year grim born

sharpening its permission

a dead man's daughter

is still next week giving herself

to california

we us diamonds broken from a larger pain

scatter

called forward

courageous

mutinous

trembling

the earth heard in a shell

our own niagara

gripped in hollow hands

pink

warm

flush with life

reaching

into the sea

hello bird

you seem a bit shy

i've never had the courage

to fly

i take these steps into

a forever

and my shoulders are sore

flinching

you seem a bit shy

my eyes only ever saw 'till nightfall

never on to morning

what's it going to take to make this right

it's me again
outside's behind some windows
sun's behind clouds partly
willing
birds
i heard them earlier
wouldn't normally have looked
honestly whatever
all this nature
has nothing to say
except as fingerprints
later these were geese on the lawn
i saw that one's neck
was longer than another's
mostly thought about them
as food

noticed how now it's normal
not strange
that some stay
throughout the year
and that i have a name
a past reflected in the glass
well worn with separation

and it's me again

looking for time

outside this skin

the glass is cold

only when touched

i thought the sun was warm

was i right

i've left 1000 times

how is it that the journey

always ends right

here

eyes a bit sadder

shoulders a bit stronger

soul a bit sleepy
when i've hidden my heart

i talked to the songbirds

it's this plague of human-ness

that really gums my wings

take-offs were always worse

than landings

high in the thermals

gliding over the sea
under faces soul between
fire licked skin
mad flapping wings
shovels of love
pitched at the breeze
city of veils
frozen tears of glass
death shattered light
grinding eyes black
these stones that filled
my pockets are free

free

like falling forever

branches scratch

face

neck

shoulders

i know secrets

that hurt my heart

and make my brain

small

i placed all this trouble

deep in my pocket

with little coins

old receipts

a forgotten fortune

and tiny yellow flowers

trouble likes to hide

so sharp a light
the sun as if an eye
in a puddle below
reflecting up
while shadows sink deeper
and light filters in between

the dark footprints
as if losings were stars
feelings blurred in other lights
while i've a body like a cradle
like roots locked in the vault of earth
perfect
brief
and darkly mingled

perfect

brief

i've pinched myself

so many times

trying to prove

existence

every hurt tells lies
about how it got there
every memory fondled
whispers far too low
i forget function
i forget duty
i forget labels
i forget
i wasn't there but was made after
when i look straight down there's nothing
marco
polo
the tail end of
screams or laughter
or the dead
was it
or the dying to be
who control the all of flowers
with their mighty silence
where were my steps

Waters

Charlevoix was but a dream now

As the breakers crashed

Over the bow

Fingers spreading

Like an enormous hand

On the deck

The Big Lake

Was just a-toyin' with us

Hollis, the old man, said

Seeming confident

Silver hair

Waves in the gale

80 years to my 8

He would tell me about the Chippewa

The Ojibwe

That prodigious tribe of nomadic warriors

And how they named her

Great Water

The red-wooden-hulled vessel

Steadfast and stalwart

Mainsail stretched tight

This is the hardest part, he shouted

Until we clear

The channel

Narrowing

Path

The

Berth

Our noble craft

Worked

From all sides

The maiden crown

South Pierhead astern

We're right in her now

Mishigami

I've never seen you desperate or speak to anyone
You wouldn't know your name, are fluid without it
Empty gate, sloppy balloon, teaching steps
To diving, floating, and to the many dead you hold
Deep recluse, a cloud who couldn't choose
Between earths. Fish swim through your hair
Drunken maniac—who said, would you, but not to me
Your bubbling counts stones on shifting shores
Across lighthouse fads—all leaves lost in your palm
The moon bobbing among thirsty blades
In the surges of your footprint, the June
The water wool, and the obstinate chill
Claiming the flats, roiling, roiling, and deep.

a single smooth stone

slick with your weather

knows you better than

all the bearded captains

and though

jealous of salt seas

i can taste your fight

deep down in my belly

when the sun cools

into your depths

and the only sense is

sound

all the whispered moments

on and under you

for even now miles away

i hear your waves inside me

M.

I've kept her secret long enough now

I am home better a week
And all it has done is rain
A mighty fine welcome back, indeed

Always telling me to go
This city
As I watch the freighters drift by, from the Isle that was Belle

The minister from the Old Mariner's church is dead
Passed in his sleep
there are no more great shipwrecks

This damn weather system
Hangs over me
My Michigan and the Lake

The steelheads have all come ashore
Last night, I sat with one, on a piece of driftwood,
next to the Grand Haven Pier
Shared some conversation, fish stories, and a smoke

I've kept her secret long enough now

None of us can let go of it

Escape her

Move beyond her shores, to the sand

Arching towards the water

The ancient cliffs, glacial till

Reach over our shoulders, under the canopy of night

We are so far behind ourselves

By the time we see its light

The star is already dead

The storm gathers again

Over the lake, blowing sparks from our beach fire

Clouds mountain on the horizon

As we stare out into the waters

Throwing the Petoskey Stone as far as we can into her hem

Casting it, a hundred years out, the old man is in my ear

The future is not so far off

H.

i've got solid oak beneath my soles
it bucks and bends to the rhythms
i don't remember where
the sea ends and my skin begins

the sun has been a father, a mother
a lover, and a thief of all i possess
and she sends her rain and wind
to play for my folly and my fortune

i've tried several times
to hang myself in the heavy clouds
but they never take my weight
and i wake back on water washed wood

i am rooted here at the great wheel
count the rings inside my limbs
brush the leaves sprouting from my skull
feel the bark covering my heartbreak

it has been 17 years 2 weeks and 1 day
since i saw my home and love
there are no more great shipwrecks
but this one will be glorious

M.

the warm breathing is as far as shore
the seed of desperate longing
to mingle

willow and her hair
streak electric her eyes
consuming lampposts as i row
a stranger to my hands
towards the sound of the saturated earth

i came from the deep
slipping through the ribbing of a sunken queen
gliding over the floor
hungry hunger burning
i mean
i wept as i bailed

onto the sturdy earth
i climb out over the bow
rope in hand
but let it fall back into the inky water
a meek sinking crease
the empty boat bobs away
is watched

the sky's where the moon used to be

camp’s been broken

it was from where

the not now stars

they've portaged

and i can’t match their speed

in this i have you

only

the earth is a tear factory

where ever feet pass

burning the souls

to again be made pure

only

the sky is laughter

where blue touches mountains

rolling down hills

to wash over me

only

these possessions are flowers

where time becomes work

to have and to have

all property: illusion

only

in this i have you

M.

they talk of a stream underground
conveying the dead
reaching from their shoulders
love's architecture
pine tops
razoring the reserve
now
in double
in triple vision
until the dim
trails in charcoal lines
"pull" called when ready
on the trigger
scatter the diamonds
before they land
the fuse of the soul lit from end to end
though all the seas have names
drowning remains the same
love lives
strikes
with dirt in our hair
houses of mud
heat
then porcelain

our shards

our sharpest edge

behind me

you have given me

behind me

by you

always in front

tell me

about

yourself

the same

as tomorrow

F.

take courage in yourself

and in the sky

is full of love

wholly

like thunder

she came to my heart

as quiet as lightning

she drifted off to sleep

barely

in my arms

in the moonbeams

mixed with candlelight

broadway looking on

solely

the rivers running

along both sides of the single bed

children's books

on the window ledge

simply

here we are stranded up high

suspended by the fear

look down the wing of the bird

soaring beside you

utterly

is full of love

and in the sky

take courage in yourself

H.

what are we worth

our weight in wounds

strips of exposed flesh

from neck to heel

another day another lash.

while you sleep

i stand before broken down cardboard

and in each hand

i hold a thousand dollars worth

designer property

i do not want

i hope

i drop

not on purpose

and break to leak and

coat the gray dust floor with

the sweet stench of emptiness

and glass

and so prove the illusion of

this whip.

while i sleep

i dream i stand before a bony face

i look down into my pouch filled with the dollar
divided by six point seven and
i look up to find
a thousand bony faces before me
waiting for
what i cannot give.

what could i give
only
that which glows in
silver lining
aligning this hot august cloud
we swim through
together.

who has bought this joy
that i may lie dizzy
in dry fan air
and drowsily
i laugh.

B.

there was smoke on the wind

like the whole sky caught flames

not even the rain came down that day

the road was dry and cracked

my wheels had worn clean slick

goodbyes stung in my eyes

and my tongue turned to brick

(but all of that was)

prelude to the river…

where are we

ambling with empty pails

under the sky

open mouthed

how we found ourselves

so wedded to danger

to between

dry earth and rain

between

light and shadow

atlas and entropy

she loves me

she loves me not

and between

ice and thaw

gravity and the grave

this pile of dust i call my fortune

cobwebs veils tombs seeds

carry me river

I got lost somehow

In these uncharted waters

My sight blurred

You were there, in that blur

I awoke in a fog

a root cellar

sheets damp

Remembering that time

when your bed was foreign

We straddled the globe

And sat aside this earth

Embracing

I wake again

Only my humble clothes are familiar

the taste of toothpaste

and this picture of you

Which I've left out to dry

R.

muscles and sinews

molded in the waves

all rivers are timelines

where did you get in?

they do not carry sorrow

they do not carry joy

grabbing branches

to slow my lurching

one branch breaks like a heart

one branch breaks like an arm

i was covered in grief

when i first hit the waters

now i'm washed clean away

exposed

vulnerable

open

to be rebuilt

assembled with love

where did you get in?

M.

There's a freighter riding high
Passing between me and Michigan
Steam-on! Go north into the arctic creep
We'll shake the spells from the blankets
And untwist our fingers from around love's throat
To re-animate, in a breath, the spark of action
in the absence of dream

Passions are mine, in a nest, in an empty attic
Calling down to their sacrifices
The tumbled basement swell
Blood rising, lake blue, aquatic birds…

I see me in the metal hull and sloppy engine
Served seconds on late watch, witness to the oily morning
Steam-on! to where the water turns solid

F.

all this around me
alive with blue
and worth nothing
on the world market
generals don't kill
for rivers anymore

all this around me
carrying my blues
a bargain bought
ticket from sorrow
generals don't kill
for justice anymore

all this around me
removed from the blue
on the wings of a hawk
sorrow looks so tiny
generals don't kill
for beauty anymore

M.

www.ingramcontent.com/pod-product-compliance
Lightning Source LLC
Chambersburg PA
CBHW031358040426
42444CB00005B/337
* 9 7 8 0 6 1 5 2 1 7 0 6 2 *